BIBLE 2
HOW YOUR BIBLE

MW01121668

CONTENTS

Author:	Iva Grant
Editor-in-Chief:	Richard W. Wheeler, M.A.Ed.
Editor:	Martha K. Baxter, M.A.Ed.
Consulting Editor:	John L. Booth, Th.D.
Revision Editor:	Alan Christopherson, M.A.

Alpha Omega Publications

300 North McKemy Avenue, Chandler, Arizona 85226-2618

ALPHA OMEGA
PUBLICATIONS

Learn with the Bridgestone characters:

When you see me, I will help your teacher explain the exciting things you are expected to do.

When you do actions with me, you will learn how to write, draw, match words, read, and much more.

You and I will learn about matching words, listening, drawing, and other fun things in your lessons.

Follow me and I will show you new, exciting truths, that will help you learn and understand what you study. Let's learn!

BIBLE

HOW YOUR BIBLE CAME TO YOU

In this LIFEPAC you are going to find out how the Bible came to be.

Some Bibles are very small.

Family Bibles are very big.

You like to carry your Bible to **church**.

All over the world people have Bibles to read.

How did this wonderful book come to be? In your Bible you can read this verse (2 Peter 1:21), ". . . holy men of God spake as they were moved by the Holy Ghost [Spirit]." This verse says that very good men wrote the Bible. They wrote what God told them to write.

You will read about these men whom God used to give you the Bible. You will read some of the things God told them.

The story about Emily, who wrote the Bible in Navajo is in this LIFEPAC. You will read about the Wycliffe **translators**. They are printing the Bible so other people can read God's **message** today.

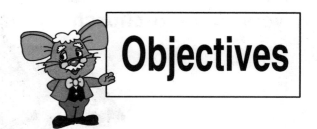

Objectives

Read these objectives. They tell you what you will be able to do when you have finished this LIFEPAC.

1. You will be able to name some holy men who wrote parts of the Bible.

2. You will be able to tell on what the Bible was written.

3. You will be able to tell how God talks to people.

4. You will be able to tell how people are being helped so everyone can have a Bible to read.

5. You will be able to name two parts of the Bible.

6. You will be able to tell about the Ten Commandments.

NEW WORDS

altar (al tar). A table or stand used in a church or the Temple for worship.

Ark. Large gold box.

bitter (bit ter). A strong taste, not a good taste.

born. To start life.

bush. A plant not as big as a tree.

charcoal (char coal). Partly burned wood.

church. A place to worship God.

cloud. A soft, floating mass in the sky.

commandment (com mand ment). One of God's rules on how to live.

copy (cop y). To write down.

cough. To force air out.

disciple (dis ci ple). A helper of Jesus.

false. Not true.

hogan (ho gan). A Navajo house.

holy (ho ly). Belonging to God.

honor (hon or). To think well of someone.

hospital (hos pi tal). A place to care for the sick.

lightning (light ning). Flash in the sky during thunderstorms.

manna (man na). Food sent by God.

message (mes sage). Words sent from one person to another.

missionary (mis sion ar y). A person sent to tell others about Jesus.

Obey (o bey). To do what one is told to do.

parchment (parch ment). An animal skin made to write on.

parents (par ents). Mother and Father.

promise (prom ise). To say you will do or not do something.

prophet (proph et)). A person who tells what will happen before it happens.

scribe. A writer.

scroll. A roll on which scribes wrote.

skin. Covering of the body.

slave. A person who belongs to another person.

special (spe cial). Different, unique.

steal. To take something that belongs to someone else.

tablet (tab let). Flat sheet of stone used to write on.

Temple (tem ple). The Jewish place to worship God.

throne. The chair of a king.

thunder (thun der). The loud noise after a flash of lightning.

tongs. A tool for picking up things.

translate (trans late). To change from one language into another language.

translator (trans lat or). A person who writes the Bible for people to read in their own language.

truth The right story.

vision (vi sion). Something seen in a dream.

worship (wor ship). To honor God.

These words will appear in **boldface** (darker print) the first time they are used.

I. HOW THE OLD TESTAMENT CAME TO YOU

The Old Testament is the first written Word of God to man. God told people what He was going to do for them. God told His people what He wanted everyone to do for Him. The Old Testament is the first part of the Bible. This part of the Bible was written before God sent Jesus to be with His people.

Two Bible stories tell how God sent messages. You will read about Moses and Isaiah. You will learn how God used these men.

WORDS TO STUDY

altar	(al tar)	A table or stand used in a church or the Temple for worship.
Ark		Large gold box.
bitter	(bit ter)	A strong taste, not a good taste.
born		To start life.
bush		A plant not as big as a tree.

church		A place to worship God.
cloud		A soft, floating mass in the sky.
commandment	(com mand ment)	One of God's rules for how to live.
false		Not true.
holy	(ho ly)	Belonging to God.
lightning	(light ning)	Flash in the sky during thunderstorms.
message	(mes sage)	Words sent from one person to another.
prophet	(proph et)	A person who tells what will happen before it happens.
scribe		A writer.
scroll		A roll on which scribes wrote on.
slave		A person who belongs to another person.
special	(spe cial)	Different, unique.
steal		To take something that belongs to someone else.

tablet	(tab let)	Flat sheet of stone used to write on.
Temple	(tem ple)	The Jewish place to worship God.
throne		The chair of a king
thunder	(thun der)	The loud noise after a flash of lightning.
tongs		A tool for picking up something.
translator	(tran slat or)	A person who writes the Bible for people to read in their own language.
truth		The right story.
vision	(vi sion)	Something seen in a dream.
worship	(wor ship)	To honor God.

SPECIAL WORDS

Isaiah	Mount Sinai
Israelite	Promised Land
Moses	

Ask your teacher to say these words with you.

Teacher Check _____
                    Initial   Date

MOSES

The Israelites had been living in Egypt for a long time. They had been **slaves** of the king.

God talked to Moses from the burning **bush**. God told Moses to go see the king. "Ask the king to let My people go," said God. Moses did not think he could do that. God told Moses that He would go with him. So Moses went to the king in Egypt. Moses asked the king to let God's people leave the country. The king did not want to listen. He wanted the Israelites to work for him.

First the king would say they could go back to their own land. Then he would say they could not go. God helped Moses. God sent many bad things to the Egyptian people. After many, many bad things were sent to them, the king let Moses and the people go.

The Israelites did what God told them to do. They left quickly so that the king could not stop them. They started walking. Moses was in front. Many men, women, children, and animals left with Moses. Moses took the people to the

Moses asked the king to let the people go.

page 8 (eight)

water. Here God helped them cross the Red Sea. The sea opened for them to cross on dry land. They were safe from the Egyptians after they had crossed the Red Sea.

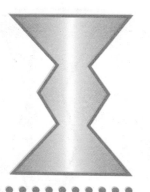

Read the sentence. Circle Yes **or** No **in front of each sentence.**

1.1   Yes   No   God wanted the king to let the people go.

1.2   Yes   No   God talked to Moses from a rock.

1.3   Yes   No   The people left Egypt slowly.

1.4   Yes   No   God helped them cross the Red Sea.

The Israelites needed food and good water to drink. They walked until they found some water. They drank the water. The water was **bitter**. It did not taste good. God said, "throw a stick in the water." Then the water tasted good.

How was God going to feed all of these people? He told them He would send food from heaven. He would send food every night. The food would be on the ground in the morning. This food tasted like cookies made with honey. It

was good! The Israelites called it **manna**.

At their next stop the Israelites looked for water again. They could not find any water. God told Moses to hit a rock with his rod. When Moses hit the rock, water came out. The people and animals drank the water.

Do this reading activity.

1.5 God sent Moses to Egypt. Moses went. Both <u>sent</u> and <u>went</u> end in <u>nt</u>. Write a word that ends in nt in each blank. Use the words in the list to help you.

rent	hunt	tent
hint	want	mint

You can live in a _____ .

Give me a _____ .

I would like a _____ to eat.

The men like to _____ .

I _____ a drink of water.

Then, from Mount Sinai, God called Moses. God said, "Tell the Israelites that I brought them out of Egypt. I brought them here. If they will do what I say, they will be My **special** people."

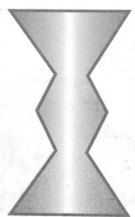
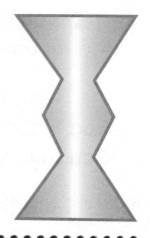

God told Moses, "I want to talk to My people. I want them to hear Me. I will come to this mountain in a **cloud**. Tell them to get ready. I will come in three days. Moses, tell the people that they must stay back from the mountain. They must not touch it."

• •

Do this reading activity.

1.6   Read these words: **after**, **first**, **burn**.
The letters **er**, **ir**, and **ur** sound like the **er** in **her**.
Write a word that has the /er/ sound in each blank.
Use the words in the list to help you.

father	thunder	burning
finger	third	mother

Moses saw a _____ bush.

God wrote on the stone with his _____ .

They saw lightning and could hear _____ from the mountain.

God said, "I will speak from the mountain on the _____ day".

Love your _____ and _____ .

• •

On the third day the people were at the mountain. Soon they heard **thunder** and saw **lightning**. They saw the cloud. It looked like the mountain was on fire.

They could see smoke. Moses went up the mountain. The people stayed back.

Then God began talking to Moses. God told him the Ten **Commandments**. God taught them,

I am the Lord your God.
You shall have no other gods before me.
You shall not have any **false** gods.
You shall love the name of the Lord, your God.
Remember to keep a day **holy**. Rest and **worship** on that day.
Love your father and your mother.
You shall not kill.
Husbands and wives should be true to each other.
You shall not **steal**.
You shall tell the **truth**.
You shall not want anything that belongs to someone else.

Learn to read the Ten Commandments. Check each box when you have finished.

1.7 ☐ Read the Ten Commandments with a friend (Exodus 20:1 through 17.)

Teacher Check _____
                Initial   Date

1.8 ☐ Read the Ten Commandments with your family.

Teacher Check _____
                Initial   Date

God loved the Israelites and wanted to help them. Because He loved His people, God gave them the Ten Commandments. The Ten Commandments were God's law.

God called Moses up into the mountain again. He gave Moses messages for His people. When Moses came down, he was carrying two tablets of stone. God had written the Ten Commandments on them.

Moses showed the stone **tablets** to the people. Moses told them all the things God wanted them to know.

· ·

Circle the word that belongs in the sentence and write the word in the blank.

1.9   Moses had done _____ God asked him to do.

        where   what

1.10   I will come to this mountain in _____ days.

        third   three

1.11   The people heard the _____.

        thirty   thunder

1.12   The mountain was _____.

        shaking   shouting

1.13   Mothers and fathers and _____
        heard God talk to Moses.
            choose   children

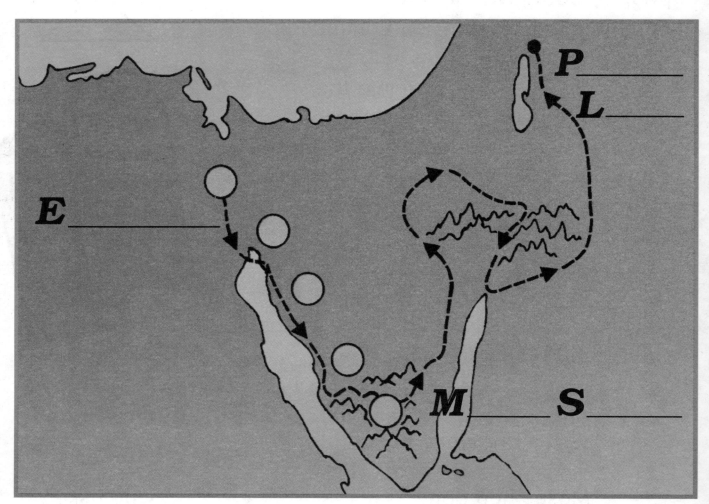

 **Do these map activities.**

1.14   The map shows where the Israelites went. A dotted
        line shows their trip. Write on the map the correct
        words. Use the words to fill in the blanks on the map.

            Egypt   Mount Sinai   Promised Land

1.15   Next, in each circle on the map write the number of the place where each thing happened:

1. Israelites left Egypt.
2. Israelites crossed the Red Sea.
3. Manna was sent.
4. Water came from a rock.
5. Ten Commandments were given.

The rest of the trip took a long time. Trace that part of the trip to the Promised Land. You may want to read more about the trip.

 Teacher Check _____
                          Initial   Date

ISAIAH

Another holy man was Isaiah. One day Isaiah had a **vision** of God in the **Temple**.

In the Temple was a holy room. In this room was an **Ark**. Holy things were kept in the Ark. Inside the Ark was some manna. The stone tablets with the Ten Commandments were in the Ark.

Isaiah saw God in his vision. He saw God sitting on a **throne**. He saw angels over the throne. They were saying, "Holy, Holy, Holy."

The room was filled with smoke. Isaiah saw fire burning on the **altar**. One of the angels went to the altar. The angel picked up a piece of hot coal with **tongs**. He put the hot coal on Isaiah's mouth.

Then Isaiah heard a voice saying, "Who will take My message to the people?"

Isaiah answered quickly, "Here am I, send me."

Do this puzzle.

1.16   Isaiah had a vision of the holy room of the Temple. The word **vision** is printed in the puzzle. Put a word from the WORD BOX in each blank. Write the words in the puzzle. Match the numbers.

1. Isaiah heard a _____ .

2. The hot coal touched his _____ .

3. Isaiah _____ the Lord.

4. Into the Temple went _____ .

5. The angels sang, "Holy, _____ , Holy."

6. "Here am I, _____ me."

WORD BOX
lips
send
saw
voice
Isaiah
Holy
Temple

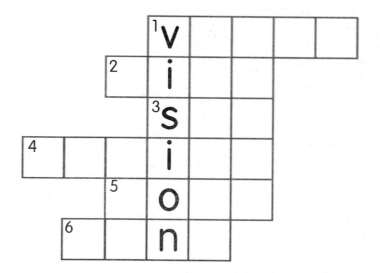

 Teacher Check _____
                        Initial   Date

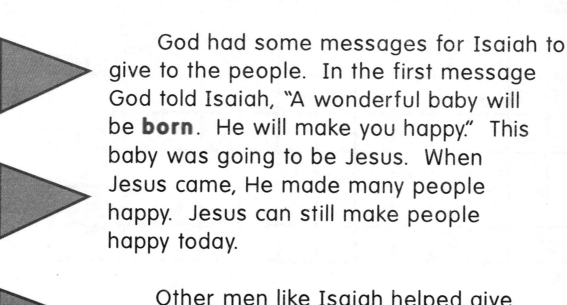

God had some messages for Isaiah to give to the people. In the first message God told Isaiah, "A wonderful baby will be **born**. He will make you happy." This baby was going to be Jesus. When Jesus came, He made many people happy. Jesus can still make people happy today.

Other men like Isaiah helped give God's message. They gave God's messages to the people. They were called **prophets**.

Do this puzzle.

1.17 Read this list of God's prophets. Write the names of these prophets in the puzzle. All of the vowels are in the puzzle for you.

Amos   Obadiah   Jeremiah   Joel
Isaiah   Hosea   Ezekiel   Daniel
Haggai   Micah

			E		E		I	A					
			E					O					
						O		E	A				
I		A	I	A									
			E			A			I		A		
	O	E						E					
						I							
			A		A	I							

Teacher Check _____
                Initial   Date

page 18 (eighteen)

God gave messages to the prophets. **Scribes** wrote the messages on **scrolls**. The scrolls were kept safe. The messages are in your Bible.

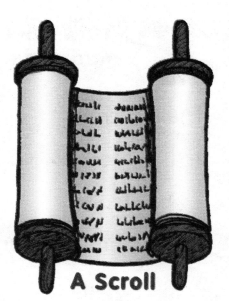

A Scroll

Make a scroll.

1.18   In the time of Jesus, people read scrolls. You can make your own scroll. It isn't hard.

> You will need these things:
>
> two sticks   glue
>
> a long paper

Follow these directions. Check each box after you finish that step.

☐   1.   Paste each end of the paper to the sticks.
☐   2.   When the paper is dry, roll the paper around the stick. Ask a friend to help you.
☐   3.   Find Second Timothy 2:15 in your Bible.
☐   4.   Write the verse on your scroll.
☐   5.   Say the verse to your friend.

Teacher Check _____
                    Initial   Date

Think about how God sent His messages.

Draw lines to match the words with the meanings.

1.19	scrolls	a writer
1.20	Moses	God gave him a message from a mountain.
1.21	Isaiah	God gave them messages for the people.
1.22	Ten Commandments	God promised to send Him.
1.23	Jesus	God gave him messages in the Temple.
1.24	prophets	messages were written on them
1.25	Old Testament	first part of the Bible
1.26	scribe	written on stone tablets

 For this Self Test, study what you have read and done. The Self Test will check what you remember.

SELF TEST 1

Draw lines to match the words to make a sentence.

1.01	You shall have	and your mother.
1.02	You shall	to worship God and rest.
1.03	You	shall not kill.
1.04	Love your father	no other gods before me.
1.05	Remember to keep a day holy	not steal.

BIBLE

2 0 4

LIFEPAC TEST

16 / 20

BIBLE 204: LIFEPAC TEST

Write a 1 in front of the sentence if it happened in the Old Testament. Write a 2 in front of the sentence if it happened in the New Testament.

1. _____ God talked to Moses from the mountain.

2. _____ God wrote the Ten Commandments on tablets of stone.

3. _____ Mark wrote about Jesus.

4. _____ Isaiah was a prophet.

5. _____ Matthew told about the storm.

6. _____ The boy gave his lunch to Jesus.

7. _____ Paul was a missionary.

8. _____ God talked to Moses.

Write the word from the WORD BOX in the blank.

WORD BOX		
Emily	Jesus	Ten
God	Moses	translated
hogan	scribes	writing
Isaiah	scrolls	

9 Men who wrote down God's messages were called

_____ .

10. Instead of in books, writing was done on

_____ .

11. The Navajo Bible was translated by _____ .

12. The _____ Commandments give us laws for our lives.

13. When we read our Bible, _____ talks to us.

14. In the Temple _____ had a vision.

15. On Mount Sinai God talked to _____ .

16. The man wrote the Bible in the words of the people. He _____ the Bible.

17. Emily lived in a Navajo home. She lived in a _____ .

18. Today Wycliffe translators are working with people. The translators are _____ the Bible for the people.

19. God talked to a holy man in the holy room. God spoke to _____ .

20. God told Isaiah that a baby would be born. God said that _____ would come.

NOTES

Circle the right answer.

1.06   The first part of the Bible is called the _____ .

oldest book   first part   Old Testament

1.07   A man who wrote on scrolls was called a _____ .

scribe   farmer   teacher

1.08   God gave the Ten Commandments to _____ .

Moses   Paul   John

1.09   God gave the message that Jesus would come to _____ .

James   Isaiah   Peter

1.010   God sent messages to the people through the _____ .

workers   prophets   scribes

8 / 10

 Teacher Check _____
Initial   Date

My Score

II. HOW THE NEW TESTAMENT CAME TO YOU

The Bible has two parts. One part was written before Jesus came to us. The first part of the Bible is the Old Testament.

The other part of the Bible was written after Jesus came. This last part of the Bible is the New Testament. The New Testament tells about Jesus.

In this part of your LIFEPAC, you will read about some of the people who wrote the New Testament. You will learn about Matthew, Mark, and Paul.

```
┌─────────────────── WORDS TO STUDY ───────────────────┐
```

copy	(cop y)	To write down.
disciple	(dis ci ple)	A helper of Jesus.
honor	(hon or)	To think well of someone.
missionary	(mis sion ar y)	A person sent to tell others about Jesus.
obey	(o bey)	To do what one is told to do.
parchment	(parch ment)	Animal skin made to write on.
parents	(par ents)	Mother and father.
promise	(prom ise)	To say you will do or not do something.
skin		Covering of the body.

Ask your teacher to say these words with you.

Teacher Check _____

Initial   Date

MATTHEW

Matthew was a man who knew Jesus. He walked with Him from town to town. The people came to Jesus. He talked to the people.

One day Jesus was teaching the people. The time was late in the day. Everyone was tired. Jesus told the people to go home. Then He said to His friends, "I see a boat on the water. Let's get in it and rest."

They got into the boat. Jesus went to the back of the boat. He fell asleep.

The boat was in the storm.

While He was sleeping, the wind began to blow. It blew so hard that the water splashed into the boat.

The men were afraid. They went back to Jesus. They woke Him up and said, "Lord, save us!"

Jesus answered, "Why are you afraid?" Then He got up and said to the wind, "Be still!" The wind stopped blowing. Everything was quiet.

Jesus' friends were surprised when He could stop the wind. They knew Jesus was a very special person.

Matthew was with Jesus that night. Matthew wrote the story. The story is in the book of Matthew. The book of Matthew is in the New Testament. You can read many other stories in Matthew's book.

- -

Print the right word in the sentence.

Track the answer from the circled letters. The first one is done for you.

This story is <u>about</u> Jesus.

s q n ⓐ l f ⓑ d e x g h n ⓞ l ⓤ s ⓣ m

2.1   They _____ Jesus asleep.

m **f** d r q n **o** m s t **u** l b **n** q r s **d** l

2.2   There was a _____ noise.

r q m n w **l** x z d **o** b n **u** l k **d** s m p

2.3   Winds blew and storm _____ came.

c d n b **l** q d z m w **o** e g **u** t l **d** **s** r

- -

MARK

Peter walked with Matthew and Jesus. Peter listened to Jesus teach. Jesus told so many things about God, the Father. The friends of Jesus told everybody what Jesus said. Peter told Mark. Mark heard

Peter tell this story. Mark wrote the story for us.

Jesus liked to sit on the ground and talk to the people. Many, many people were listening. The time was late. The people were hungry.

A **disciple** said, "We must send these people away. We cannot feed all of them."

Jesus said, "No, we will give them something to eat. Bring some food to me."

- -

 Write the spoken words.

2.4 Read the story from Mark. Find the words spoken by the disciple and by Jesus. Print the words in the balloons beside the right pictures.

People came to Jesus.

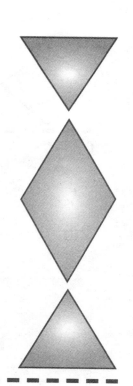

One disciple found a little boy with a lunch. The boy had five pieces of bread and two fish. The disciple said to the little boy, "Will you give your lunch to Jesus?"

The boy answered, "Yes. I will give my lunch to Jesus."

Write the spoken words.

2.5   Write the words of the disciples in the balloon beside the disciple's head. Write the words of the boy in the balloon beside the boy's head.

The boy has a lunch.

The disciples and the boy took the lunch to Jesus. Jesus broke up the bread and fish. Jesus thanked God for the food.

Jesus said, "Thank you, dear God, for this lunch.

 Write the spoken words.

2.6 Write the words of Jesus in the balloon.

_____

_____

Jesus thanks God.

The disciples gave the bread and fish to all the people. Everyone ate all they wanted. The food was never gone. From the little boy's lunch, Jesus fed everyone.

The disciples said, "We have twelve baskets of food left." Do you think they gave one basket to the little boy?

Write the spoken words.

2.7   Write the words of the disciples in the balloon
       beside the heads of the disciples.

Twelve baskets of food were left.

 Teacher Check _____
                        Initial   Date

 **Do these activities.**

2.8   Circle the words that end like **boy**.
       I heard about a little boy.
       I think his name was Roy.
       He gave his lunch to Jesus.
       And he was filled with joy.

2.9   Put **oi** in these words. Say them to your helper.
       t ___ ___ l   j ___ ___ n   c ___ ___ l   s ___ ___ l

       sp ___ ___ l   c ___ ___ n   p ___ ___ nt   b ___ ___ l

Teacher Check _____
                  Initial   Date

page 29 (twenty-nine)

PAUL

God used Paul to help give messages to the people of the world. Paul was a **missionary**—a person who tells people about Jesus. He was the very first missionary. He would go to a city and visit the churches there. Then he would go to another city. He would preach in the churches he had visited.

Sometimes Paul wrote the letters himself. Sometimes a scribe would write the letters for him. The scribes wrote with a pen on **parchment**.

Parchment was made from animal **skins**. The skins were cleaned. The hair was taken off. Then the skins were pulled very hard. The skins were pulled until they were as thin as paper. When the thin skins were dry, the scribes could write on them.

The scribes **copied** Paul's letters. The scribes were very careful to copy them correctly.

Do this Bible activity.

2.10   Write these names under the part of the Bible where you would find them.

Paul   Isaiah   Peter   Moses

Jesus   Matthew   Mark

Old Testament   **New Testament**

_____   _____

_____   _____

_____   _____

_____   _____

_____   _____

Paul wrote a letter to the children of one church. Read what Paul wrote (Ephesians 6:1 through 3).

Children, obey your parents in the Lord: for this is right. Honour thy father and mother; which is the first commandment with promise; That it may be well with thee, and thou mayest live long on the earth.

Do you **obey** your **parents**? If you obey them, you **honor** them. God has **promised** to all children who obey their parents that life will go well for them. He has promised that they will live many years on earth.

Learn a Bible verse. Learn Ephesians 6:1 through 3. Say the verse to a friend. Say the verse to your family.

Teacher Check _____

Print the answers in the blanks.

2.11 Here are some mixed-up words. Find the one that belongs in the sentence and write it on the line.

Lrsttee   chchesur   aimlan

beoy   ssribec

Paul visited the _____.

Paul wrote the _____.

Parchment is made from _____ skins.

The _____ would copy Paul's letter.

Children, _____ your parents.

God used all of these people to write the Bible. As you look in your Bible, you will see many books. God helped someone write each book.

God talks to you when you read the Bible. You must read the Bible every day. Then every day He will tell you His message.

Study what you have read and done for this Self Test. This Self Test will check what you remember of this part and other parts you have read.

SELF TEST 2

Circle Yes **or** No.

2.01	Matthew walked with Jesus from town to town.	Yes	No
2.02	The men went for a ride in a car.	Yes	No
2.03	Jesus told the wind, "Be still."	Yes	No
2.04	Mark was a friend of Peter.	Yes	No
2.05	The little boy kept his lunch.	Yes	No

Write the correct word in the sentence.

2.06   Paul was a _____ .
          message   missionary

2.07   The scribes wrote on _____ .
          paper   parchment

2.08   Matthew is a book in the _____ .
          Old Testament   New Testament

2.09   God gave us the Bible through _____ men.
          holy   holly

2.010   The Bible is a _____ from God.
          letter   bitter

Find the word in the WORD BOX that belongs in the sentence. Write the word in the sentence.

2.011   A prophet gives the people God's _____ .

2.012   God told Isaiah that Jesus would be _____ .

2.013   Isaiah heard God's _____ .

2.014   A commandment is a _____ .

2.015   God sent manna from _____ .

WORD BOX

Jesus

law

heaven

voice

message

born

12/15 Teacher Check _____

Initial   Date

My Score

• •

III. HOW THE BIBLE COMES TO PEOPLE TODAY

Some people do not have a Bible they can read. Translators help these people. The translators listen to the people to learn how they say their words. Then the translators write the Bible so that the people can read it.

This story is true. This story is about a translator named Emily. She is writing the Bible so that Navajo Indians can read it.

WORDS TO STUDY

cough		To force air out.
hogan	(ho gan)	A Navajo home.
hospital	(hos pi tal)	A place to care for the sick.
translate	(trans late)	To change into another way of speaking

SPECIAL WORDS

Navajo   Wycliffe

Ask your teacher to say these words with you.

Teacher Check _____
                    Initial   Date

EMILY, THE NAVAJO GIRL

Emily was a little Navajo girl. She had a brother and a sister. In the summer they watched the sheep.

Emily liked to watch the sheep because it was a good time to play. She played with rocks and sticks and mud. She made sheep and goats out of mud. She made little **hogans** out of sticks and mud. Summer was a happy time.

A Navajo home is called a hogan.

When summer was over school began again. Emily begged her mother to let her go to school. Emily was little, but her mother let Emily go to school. School time was another happy time. Emily loved school.

When Emily was in the fifth grade, she got sick. Emily had a bad **cough**. The cough did not get any better. When Emily was in the eighth grade, she had to go to the **hospital**. Emily was so sad. She wanted to go to school. She did not want to be in the hospital.

One day a lady came to see Emily in the hospital. This lady was a missionary. The missionary had a book called the Bible. Emily had never seen a Bible. She started to read the stories in the Bible.

Emily liked school.

She read about Jesus. Emily had another happy time. Reading about Jesus' love made her happy. Jesus loved Emily and made her feel better.

When Emily felt better she went

home. Then she said, "I wish my people could read a Bible in Navajo."

She wrote about Jesus in Navajo. She found some Navajo friends to help her. They worked a long time. They translated the Bible into Navajo.

This is the way John 20:21 looks in the Navajo Bible:

Ndi Jesus ei Christ, Diyin God biYe niliigo deidoohdlaaligii biniye diidiigii bik i ndahaasdzo ako ei deinohdlaago bada iinohliigo hazhi bibiit aa iina nihee daholoo dooleel.

Emily is still writing in Navajo. She writes songs and stories. Emily works hard so that Navajo people can know about God's love for them. Telling about God's love to her people makes her very happy.

Write John 20:31.

3.1   Use your Bible.

_____

- -

_____

Teacher Check _____

Initial   Date

WYCLIFFE TRANSLATORS

You have read about Emily. Emily is a missionary. She wrote the words of Jesus in Navajo. The people who speak Navajo can now read the Bible.

Many men and women are helping to bring the Bible to other people. The Wycliffe translators go to other places in the world. They take God's message to different people. The translators write the Bible in the language of the people.

First, the Wycliffe translators go to live with the people. They learn how to talk like the people. Next, the translators match letters they know with the sounds the people use. Then, the letters are put together to make words. The words are used to write the Bible in the way the people talk.

Someone teaches the people how to read. The people can then read the Bible. The people have their own Bible to read. The Wycliffe translators are bringing God's message to many people today.

Write the missing words in the blanks.

3.2   Emily's family had _____ boy(s) and
_____ girl(s) in it.

3.3   In the summer Emily _____ the sheep.

3.4   Emily's _____ let her go to school.

3.5   Emily was sick with a _____ .

3.6   The home of a Navajo is a _____ .

3.7   Emily wrote the _____ in Navajo.

3.8   The _____ translators are writing
the Bible in words people can read.

Write a sentence using each word.

3.9   translate

_____

3.10   holy

_____

3.11   message

_____

3.12   commandments

_____

3.13   manna

_____

3.14   honor

_____

Study what you have read and done for this last Self Test. This Self Test will check what you remember in your studies of all parts in this LIFEPAC. The last Self Test will tell you what parts of the LIFEPAC you need to study again.

SELF TEST 3

Draw lines to match the words.

3.01   commandments   Navajo house

3.02   obey   honor God

3.03   honor   laws

3.04   worship   do what one is told

3.05   hogan   love

Write one of these words in each blank.

sister   better   summer   mother   brother

3.06   When _____ was over, it was time for school to begin.

3.07   Another boy in the family is called a _____ .

3.08   Emily's cough did not get _____ .

3.09   Another girl in the family is called a _____ .

3.010   Emily begged her _____ to let her
         go to school.

Draw a line under the sentences that are true.

3.011   God used holy men to give us the Bible.

3.012   God wrote the Ten Commandments.

3.013   The Old Testament is the last part of the Bible.

3.014   The Temple has a holy room.

3.015   Manna tasted like apples.

12/15   Teacher Check _____
                      Initial   Date   **My Score**

         Before taking the LIFEPAC Test, you should do
these self checks.

1.   Did you do good work
      on your last Self Test?

2.   Did you study again those parts of the LIFEPAC
      you did not remember?
      Check one: ☐ Yes (good)
                    ☐ No (ask your teacher)

3.   Do you know all the new words in "Words to
      Study"?
      Check one: ☐ Yes (good)
                    ☐ No (ask your teacher)

ALPHA OMEGA
PUBLICATIONS

Chandler, Arizona
1-800-622-3070
www.home-schooling.com

BIB0204-Jul '00 Printing

ISBN 0-86717-114-6

NB21

9 780867 171143

99000